THE LETTERS OF NESTORIUS

Nestorius,

Archbishop of Constantinople

Translated by: D.P. Curtin

Dalcassian Publishing Company

PHILADELPHIA, PA

Copyright @ 2023 Dalcassian Publishing Company

All rights reserved. No part of this publication may be reproduced, distributed, or transmitted in any form or by any means, including photocopying, recording, or other electronic or mechanical methods, without the prior written permission of the publisher, except in the case of brief quotations embodied in critical reviews and certain other non-commercial uses permitted by copyright law. For permission request, write to Dalcassian Publishing Company at dalcassianpublishing at gmail.com

ISBN: 979-8-8689-9170-7 (Paperback)

Library of Congress Control Number:
Author: Curtin, D.P. (1985-)

Printed by Ingram Content Group, 1 Ingram Blvd, La Vergne, Tennessee

First printing edition 2023.

ADMINISTRATION IN THE THREE FOLLOWING EPISTLES.

By Fr. Jacques Migne

Two things seem to me to be inquired about these three epistles: the second, whether they have a definite author; the other, by which interpreter they were turned into Latin speech. By right, no one can doubt that they were all written by Nestorius, although there is no Greek text by anyone; for they were mentioned by Celestinus, Cyril, Cassianus, and Marius Mercator, whose authority makes sure belief.

Celestine to the clergy and people of Constantinople (*1 P. Conc. Ephes. 19*): "Nestorius preaches abominable things about the virgin birth and the divinity of Christ our God and Savior, forgetting, as it were, his reverence and the common salvation of all, and persuades them to be avoided, just as his writings transmitted to us by him, with his own signature, as also the report of my holy brother and co-bishop Cyril, sent to me by the son of Possidonius the deacon, and revealed to me." And to John of Antioch (*Ibid., 20*): "These things have come to us through the sorrow of the faithful. These were published in books which he himself had sent. And what is a greater proof, these things have been insinuated in the letters sent to us, secured by the signature of the author himself, so that it is no longer permissible to doubt." And to Nestorius himself (Ibid., ch. 18): "We received your letters a long time ago, to which we could give no answer in the narrowness of the situation." For they were to be translated into Latin speech: "what when, though late, we do, etc." And a little later: "Now considering, and the complaint against you of the aforesaid brother, and finally interpreting your letters, containing open blasphemy."

Cyril speaking to John the Ancient of Nestorius (*Ibid., 21*): "I had advised him by letter to abstain from those wicked and perishing questions, and to follow the faith of the Fathers: but thinking that I had written these things out of hatred, he was so absent that he had no reason at all for it who had prescribed these things to his piety out of charity, so that, feeling thus, and saying thus, they might insinuate themselves into the ears of the Romans also, and hope to preoccupy them [...] mass, among other things against those who dissent from him," he also added these things, "They call the lyre a horror, the sacred Virgin, the mother of God (*Epist. 1:4*)." In addition to these, he also sent some quatrains of his exegesis, etc. And a little later: "Having read the epistles in the council, and especially those in which there can be no room for sycophancy; for they contain his signature." And to Juvenal (*Ibid., 24*): "But having decided that he could attract the Roman Church to his opinion, he wrote to my lord Celestinus, and in these letters inserted the perversity of his dogmas; He also sent many exegetes, etc."

Cassianus (*Book I, On the Incarnation 3*): For this is the reason why he encourages the complaints of the Pelagianists by his intercessions, and by his writings help their causes. And in another place (*Book II:2*): You say therefore, whoever you are, a heretic, who denies that God was born of a virgin, Mary the mother of our Lord Jesus Christ Θεοτόκον, that is, she cannot be called the mother of God, but Χριστοτόκον that is, Only the mother of Christ, not of God. "For no one," you say, "gives birth to an older man" (*Epistle 1:5*). And again in another place (Book 7:7): "But the second of your perversity is either blasphemous slander, or slanderous blasphemy, because you say, "The birth of a parent must be ὁμούσιος," not unlike the first. For it is different in words rather than in matter and kind: for when it comes to the birth of God, you say the same thing, "a more powerful man could not have been born from Mary," as above (Epistle 1:4), "an earlier man could not have been begotten."

It is certain that the third letter was given by Marius Mercator in Latin. The question can only concern the first two, whether they had an interpreter Cassianus, or Dionysius the Lesser, or someone else.

For Marius, there is a great similarity of the Latin between the second and third letters. He also makes that sentence, that they mortify the Only Begotten Deity in the flesh, etc., to be found in the same words existing in the letters of Cyril to the clerics of Constantinople, which Marius interpreted; he does, in short, that in them the voices otherwise familiar to Mario are usurped, the predication, the predicated, etc.

But it is for Cassian that he read the same letters sent by St. Leo to the archdeacon; and indeed at the time when S. Celestinus wrote the interpretation; that he also relates fragments from them, expressed in no other words than those which are now being read.

It is perhaps he who gives this version to Dionysius the Short, relying, as he seems to himself, on the testimony both of Cassiodorus and of Dionysius himself. For he wrote that the Council of Ephesus was given Latin by Dionysius. Here he insinuates that the faith of Cyril and the impiety of Nestorius were unknown to the Latins until his own time, and that for this reason he undertook to interpret Cyril's synod.

It is true that letters of this kind have been given in Latin in the year 430 AD, and indeed 429 AD, since even the supreme pontiff writes the verses before his reply to the letters of Nestorius, and the complete sentences are read in the work of Cassian, which was elaborated in these times, Dionysius, however, is a whole century later, for he lived 533 AD. Then Cassiodorus, as also Isidorus Mercator, in the name of the Council of Ephesus understood only the synodical letter of Cyril, with twelve anathemas. Finally, when Dionysius flourished after the fifth synod itself, at which time Ephesus had already long since become Latin, he either slipped through thoughtlessness when he wrote the above, or he looked to the impiety of Nestorius, which was reviving in his time.

Leaving aside this opinion, therefore, I would willingly incline to the side of Cassian, unless the lowliness of speech, which is found in these Latin epistles, would seem to be not quite in harmony with the loftiness and grandeur of the speech, which shines forth in the seven books of the Incarnation, and also in those fragments which are from the speeches of Nestorius Cassianus in Latin; nor do the two sentences which have been adduced to the contrary sufficiently prove the matter in question, for they are rendered verbatim from the Greek, how it is equally expressed by all in the same words.

Nor do I think they were translated by Mercator, indeed, when they were translated. He was engaged in Constantinople, where he presented the Commonitorium to the emperor 429 AD, under his death. It remains, therefore, that the Latin text are said to have been made by another unknown person: yet this does not prevent them from being referred to this place; for although the two former in manuscripts not being found in our codices, I thought that the third should nevertheless be added, on account of the kinship of the subject; and to be edited better than before, so that they may be understood by the readers; and to be placed in the common volume of the Works of Nestorius, that it may serve for the convenience of some learned men.

THE EPISTLE OF NESTORIUS TO THE BLESSED POPE OF THE CITY OF ROME.

1. We owe each other fraternal conversations, as if (truly between us, according to the Scriptures, obtaining concord) we would fight against the devil, the enemy of peace. Why this anti-speech? A certain Julian, and Florus, and Orontius, and Fabius, saying that they were bishops of the Western parts, often went to the most pious and preached emperor, and lamented their causes, as if the orthodox had suffered persecution in orthodox times. Often lamenting the same things with us, and often being rejected, they did not stop doing the same, but persisted day by day, filling everyone's ears with tearful voices.

2. Indeed, we are assailed by these words with which it was necessary, since we did not know the true faith of their business; but since we need a more open knowledge of their causes, lest our most pious and most Christian emperor should often endure trouble from them, lest we, ignorant of their causes, be divided about the defense of the business, should deign to give us knowledge of them; lest some, being ignorant of the justice of the truth, should be disturbed by an intrusive pity, or the canonical indignation of your beatitude, which may have been proved against them for sects of religion, esteem something else than this. For the novelty of the sects deserves no defense from the true shepherds.

LETTERS OF NESTORIUS

3. Wherefore we also, finding not a little corruption of orthodoxy among some here, and daily use anger and gentleness towards the sick. For it is not a small disease, but akin to the putrefaction of Apollinaris and Arius. For the Sunday union in man will be mixed here and there to a certain confusion of moderation: so much so that some of our clerics, some of whom from incompetence, others from heretical fraud once hidden in themselves (such as happened to many in the times of the apostles), become ill like heretics, and openly blaspheme God, The Word, Father, ὁμούσιον, as if it had taken its origin from the Virgin Χριστοτόκῳ, was built within her temple, and was buried in the flesh; they say that the same flesh did not remain after the resurrection, but passed into the nature of the Deity. To sum up, they refer to the Deity of the Only Begotten, and to the origin of the conjoined flesh, and mortify the flesh; but they blaspheme that the flesh joined to the Deity has passed to the Deity, using the very word of Deification, which is nothing else but to corrupt both.

4. But even the Virgin Κριστοτόκον has been ventured by some to say; but those who call this Θεοτόκον are not horrified, when those saints and above all preaching the Fathers at Nicaea are read to have said nothing more about the holy Virgin, except that our Lord Jesus Christ was incarnated from the Holy Spirit and the virgin Mary: and I am silent in the Scriptures, which everywhere call the Virgin the mother of Christ. not of the Word of God, and they preached through angels and apostles.

5. Because of the many struggles we endured, I esteem that the previous report taught your blessedness, also attending to this fact that we did not struggle in vain, but that many of those who were perverse were corrected by the grace of the Lord, learning from us that the birth of a parent must be ὁμούσιος; because there is no mixture of the Word of God with man, but the union of the creature and humanity of the Lord, united to God from the Virgin through the Spirit.

6. But if anyone proposes this name Θεοτοκον, because of the born humanity united to God the Word, and not because of the one who gave birth, we say indeed that this term is not suitable for her who gave birth. For the true mother must be of the same essence from which he was born; however, it can be carried

because of the consideration itself, and that this word is only mentioned about the Virgin because the temple of God the Word is inseparable from her, not because she is the mother of God the Word; for no one begets himself older.

7. Indeed, I think that this signified the preceding report; but we also explain what has happened, and we show by facts that with a brotherly spirit we desire to know the business of those whom we have predicted, not with the desire of intrusive curiosity, while we also narrate our own, as brothers to brothers, publishing to each other the novelty of the sects, so that it may be to me the truest source of literature: for I said, when I began these letters, because we owe each other fraternal conversations. I and those who are with me greet all who are with you in brotherhood in Christ.

THE EPISTLE II OF NESTORIUS TO THE BLESSED POPE

1. I have often written to your beatitude on account of Julian, Orontius, and the rest, who usurp to themselves the episcopal dignity, and make the most frequent additions to the most pious and preached emperor, and fall upon us with frequent lamentations, as if in orthodox times they had been thrown from the West. But until now we have received no writings about these from your veneration: which if I had, I could answer them, and give a concise answer to their voices. For now, from their uncertain sayings, no one has anything to turn to: others calling them heretics and saying that they were therefore projected from the Western parts; but swearing by themselves, that they had endured slander, and suffered danger for the orthodox faith by stealth. Of whom it is certain, our ignorance is grievous: for to sympathize with them, if they are really heretics, is a crime; and again, not to sympathize, if they bear slander, is harsh and impious.

2. Therefore, your most loving soul of God is worthy to inform us, who have hitherto been divided on both points, that is, both to their hatred and to their pity; but we want to be taught how to hold an opinion about them. For we separate the same men every day, disguising themselves, in the hope and expectation of your happiness.

3. For, O most venerable one, as you know, the discussion of a pious sect is not a cheap thing: nor is the trial of those who do this a small thing. For we have a great deal of work to do here, while we work to remove the sordid impiety of the worst opinion of Apollinaris and Arius concerning the Church of God. to the deity of the Only-Begotten, and the immutability of the Deity passed over to the nature of the body, and they confound both natures (which are worshiped by the supreme and unconfused conjunction in one person of the Only-Begotten) with the changeability of conformity.

4. The blind, who neither remember the exposition of those holy Fathers, nor see, protest openly against them: We believe in one Lord Jesus Christ, the Son

of God, incarnate from the Holy Spirit and the virgin Mary. For this word, to the Lord, signifies both natures; indeed, Christ is the ὁμούσιος of the Father's deity: humanity, however, born of the holy Virgin in later times, is worshiped at the same time by angels and men because of the conjunction of deity.

5. He, then, who here is weary with so many labors because of the perversity of the sects, consider what he must again suffer, if he does not know the business of the aforesaid men, and fears too much, lest through ignorance he should add to the heretics placed here. Wherefore I beseech you, that he may be on all sides devoted to your holy soul, to give notice of the aforesaid men: especially since the most faithful sequester of letters, Valerius the chamberlain, may by himself explain their troubles to your beatitude. All the brotherhood in Christ that is with you, I and those who are with me, we salute most.

EPISTLE III OF NESTORIUS, WRITING BACK TO CELESTIUM.

Greetings in the Lord to the honorable and most pious priest Coelstius, from Nestorius.

1. Do not bear it painfully, venerable one, by bearing it from those who must do what is brought upon them, and above all those who assert the truth, and those who flee from the communion of the polluted or contaminated: because even the saints who existed before our age were happy with sufferings; and they were indeed temporal, but the truth was eternal. Thus, John the Baptist, accusing Herod of sin, and indeed the existing king, was condemned by the head; but he was not afraid, for Christ had a head that could not be cut off. Thus, Paul and Peter were also killed in this way. And what more needs to be said? Thus, it has always been done, running through various temptations with piety.

2. Do not, therefore, fall short of the truth and betray it (since the letters sent to the bishops from the Western Council and from Alexandria, written by many, make our opinion clear to us), that is to wise men of the same orthodox profession: for perhaps something useful will come to the Churches of the right faith, cooperating with the Lord. We salute all the fraternity.

And with another hand: With a safe and strong heart, and much praying for us, you give us, most religious brother.

LATIN TEXT

IN TRES EPISTOLAS SEQUENTES ADMONITIO.

Duo mihi quaerenda videntur de tribus istis epistolis: alterum, an certum habeant auctorem; alterum, a quo interprete versae sint in Latinum sermonem.

Jure nemo dubitare potest quin omnes a Nestorio scriptae sint reipsa, quamvis nullius habeatur textus Graecus; earum enim meminerunt Coelestinus, Cyrillus, Cassianus et Marius Mercator, quorum auctoritas certam facit fidem.

Coelestinus ad clerum populumque Constantinopolitanum (I p. conc. Ephes. cap. 19): Nestorius de virgineo partu et de divinitate Christi Dei et Salvatoris nostri, velut ejus reverentiae et communis omnium salutis oblitus, nefanda praedicat, vitanda persuadet, sicut et ejus scripta ad nos ab ipso, cum propria subscriptione, transmissa, sicut etiam relatio sancti fratris et coepiscopi mei Cyrilli per filium Possidonium diaconum, ad me missa patefecit. Et ad Joannem Antiochenum (Ibid., cap 20): Haec ad nos, ingerente dolore fidelium, pervenerunt. Haec libris, quos ipse miserat, publicata sunt. Et quod majoris probationis est, haec ad nos missis epistolis, ipsa auctoris subscriptione munitis, ita insinuata sunt, ut dubitare ultra non liceat. Et ad ipsam Nestorium (Ibid., cap. 18): Dudum sumpsimus epistolas tuas, quibus in angusto nihil potuimus dare responsi. Erant enim in Latinum sermonem vertendae: quod cum, licet sero, facimus, etc. Et paulo post: Nunc considerantes, et querelam de te praedicti fratris, et interpretatas tandem epistolas tuas, apertam blasphemiam continentes.

Cyrillus ad Joannem Anticchenum de Nestorio loquens (Ibid., cap. 21): Consulueram ipsi per litteras, ut abstineret a pravis illis periersisque quaestionibus, et Patrum fidem sequeretur: verum ratus haec me ex odio scripsisse, tantum abfuit ut ullam omnino rationem habuerit illius qui haec ad ejus pietatem ex charitate praescripserat, ut ita sentiens, et ita dicens, in Romanorum quoque aures insinuare se posse, easdemque praeoccupare speravent [...]Etenim prolixa epistola absurda quaedam dogmata complevus, eaque ad dominum meum Coelestinum piissimum Ecclesiae Romanae episcopum missa, inter caetera adversus illos qui ab ipso dissentiunt haec quoque adjecit, "Citra horrorem sacram Virginem Dei genitricem appellant (Epist. 1 part. IV)." Misit praeter haec, et quosdam quoque suarum exegeseon quaterniones, etc. Et paulo post: Lectis in concilio epistolis, iisque maxime in quibus non potest esse locus sycophantiae; continent enim ejus subscriptionem. Et ad Juvenalem (Ibid., cap. 24): Arbitratus autem se posse Romanam Ecclesiam in suam sententiam attrahere, scripsit ad dominum meum Coelestinum, hisque litteris suorum dogmatum perversitatem inseruit; misit quoque multas exegeses, etc.

Cassianus (Lib. I de Incarn. cap. 3): Hinc enim illud est quod intercessionibus suis Pelagianistarum querelas fovet, et scriptis suis causas illorum adjuvat. Et alio in loco (Lib. II cap. 2): Dicis itaque quisquis es ille, haeretice, qui Deum ex virgine natum negas, Mariam matrem Domini nostri Jesu Christi Θεοτόκον, id est, matrem Dei appellari non posse, sed Χριστοτόκον id est, Christi tantum matrem, non Dei. « Nemo enim, inquis, antiquiorem se parit (Epist. 1 part. 5). » Et alio iterum loco (Lib. VII cap. 7): Secunda autem perversitatis tuae, vel calumnia blasphematrix, vel blasphemia calumniatrix est, quia ais, "ὁμούσιος Parienti debet esse nativitas," non dissimilis superiori. Verbis enim magis quam re et genere diversa est: cum enim de nativitate Dei agatur, idem dicis, "potentiorem ex Maria non potuisse nasci," quod superius (Epist. 1 part. IV), "anteriorem non potuisse generari".

Certum est tertiam epistolam a Mario Mercatore Latinitate donatam; quaestio ad solas priores duas pertinere potest, an Cassianum interpretem habuerint, an Dionysium Exiguum, an alium quemcumque.

Pro Mario facit magna similitudo Latinitatis inter has epistolas duas et tertiam: facit etiam, quod ea sententia, Deitatem Unigeniti commortificant carni, etc., reperiatur iisdem verbis in litteris Cyrilli ad clericos Constantinopoli existentes, quas Marius interpretatus est; facit denique quod in iis usurpentur voces alioquin Mario familiares, praedicatio, praedicatissimus, etc.

At pro Cassiano est quod easdem epistolas a S. Leone tunc archidiacono missas legerit; et eo quidem tempore, quo S Coelestinus scribit interpretatas; quod item ex eis referat fragmenta, non aliis expressa verbis quam quae nunc leguntur.

Esset fortasse qui Dionysio Exiguo hanc versionem tribueret, fretus, ut sibi videretur, testimonio tum Cassiodori, tum ipsiusmet Dionysii. Ille enim a Dionysio concilium Ephesinum Latinitate donatum scripsit; hic insinuat Cyrilli fidem et Nestorii impietatem ad sua usque tempora Latinis ignoratam fuisse, eaque de causa se suscepisse interpretandam Cyrilli synodicam.

Verum Latinitate donatae sunt ejusmodi epistolae, ann. 430, immo 429, quandoquidem et summus pontifex versas scribit ante suam responsionem ad litteras Nestorii, et sententiae integrae leguntur in opere Cassiani, quod his temporibus elaboratum est, Dionysius tamen uno toto saeculo posterior est, vixit enim ann. 533. Deinde Cassiodorus, quemadmodum et Isidorus Mercator, nomine concilii Ephesini solam intellexit epistolam synodicam Cyrilli, cum duodecim anathematismis. Denique Dionysius, cum floruerit post ipsam quoque quintam synodum, quo tempore jam dudum Ephesina Latina facta erat, aut per incogitantiam verbo lapsus est, cum superiora scriberet, aut ad reviviscentem suis temporibus Nestorii impietatem respexit.

Hac igitur opinione praetermissa, inclinarem libens in partes Cassiani, nisi humilitas dictionis, quae in his epistolis Latinis reperitur, videretur non satis convenire cum excelsitate et granditate sermonis, quae elucet in libris septem de Incarnatione, atque etiam in fragmentis illis quae ex sermonibus Nestorii Cassianus Latina fecit; neque vero quae in contrarium allatae sunt sententiae duae satis probant rem qua de agitur, nam ex Graeco verbatim redditae sunt, quomodo ab omnibus par est iisdem vocibus exprimi.

Neque etiam a Mercatore versas puto, siquidem tunc cum verterentur. Constantinopoli versabatur, ubi Commonitorium obtulit imperatori ann. 429, sub finem. Restat igitur ut ab alio ignoto Latinae factae dicantur: neque tamen id obsistit quominus in hunc locum referendae fuerint; nam etsi duae priores in mss. codicibus nostris non inveniantur, tertiae nihilominus adjungendas ratus sum, propter cognationem argumenti; et edendas emendatiores quam prius, ut possint a lectoribus intelligi; et in commune volumen Operum Nestorii reponendas, ut nonnulli eruditorum commoditati serviatur.

EPISTOLA I NESTORII AD COELESTINUM PAPAM URBIS ROMAE.

1. Fraternas nobis invicem debemus collocutiones, velut (vera inter nos, secundum Scripturas, obtinente concordia) pugnaturi in diabolum pacis inimicum. Quorsum hoc antiloquium? Julianus quidam, et Florus, et Orontius, et Fabius dicentes se Occidentalium partium episcopos, saepe et piissimum et praedicatissimum imperatorem adierunt, ac suas causas defleverunt, tamquam orthodoxi orthodoxis temporibus persecutionem passi. Saepe eadem et apud nos lamentantes, ac saepe rejecti, eadem facere non desierunt, sed insistunt per dies singulos, implentes aures omnium vocibus lacrymosis.

2. His quidem ad eos sermonibus quibus oportuit asi sumus, cum negotii eorum veram fidem nesciremus; sed quoniam apertiore nobis de causis eorum notitia opus est, ne piissimus et christianissimus imperator noster molestiam saepe ab his sustineat, ne nos, ignorantes eorum causas, circa negotii defensionem dividamur, dignare nobis de his notitiam largiri; ne vel quidam, ignorando justitiam veritatis, importuna commiseratione conturbentur, vel canonicam indignationem beatitudinis tuae, quae contra eos pro sectis religionis forte probata est, aliud quiddam quam hoc aestiment. Nam sectarum novitas nullam meretur defensionem a veris pastoribus.

3. Unde et nos non modicam corruptionem orthodoxiae apud quosdam hic reperientes, et ira et lenitate circa aegros quotidie utimur. Est enim aegritudo non parva, sed affinis putredinis Apollinaris et Arii. Dominicam enim in homine unionem ad cujusdam contemperationis confusionem passim commiscent: adeo ut et quidam apud nos clerici, quorum alii ex imperitia, alii ex haeretica fraude in se olim celata (qualia plurima et apostolorum temporibus contigerunt) tamquam haeretici aegrotent, et aperte blasphement, Deum Verbum Patri ὁμούσιον, tamquam originis initium de Χριστοτόκῳ Virgine

sumpsisset, cum templo suo aedificatum esse, et carni consepultum; eamdem carnem dicunt post resurrectionem non mansisse, sed in naturam transiisse Deitatis. Ut in compendio dicam, Deitatem Unigeniti, et ad originem conjunctae carnis referunt, et commortificant carni; carnem vero conjunctam Deitati ad Deitatem transiisse blasphemant, usi ipso verbo Deificationis, quod nihil est aliud nisi utrumque corrumpere.

4. Sed et Virginem Κριστοτόκον ausi sunt modo quidam dicere; hanc vero Θεοτόκον vocantes non perhorrescunt, quando sancti illi et supra omnem praedicationem Patres per Nicaeam nihil amplius de sancta Virgine dixisse leguntur, nisi quia Dominus noster Jesus Christus incarnatus est ex Spiritu sancto et Maria virgine: et taceo Scripturas, quae ubique Virginem matrem Christi, non Dei Verbi, et per angelos, et per apostolos praedicarunt.

5. Propter quae quanta certamina sustinuerimus, aestimo famam praecedentem docuisse beatitudinem tuam, hoc quoque attendentem quod non frustra certaverimus, sed emendati sint gratia Domini multi ex his qui perversi erant, discentes a nobis quia debet esse parienti ὁμούσιος nativitas; quia Dei Verbi commixtura nulla est cum homine, sed unio creaturae et humanitatis Dominicae Deo conjunctae ex Virgine per Spiritum.

6. Si quis autem hoc nomen Θεοτοκον, propter natam humanitatem conjunctam Deo Verbo, non propter parientem proponat, dicimus quidem hoc vocabulum in eam quae peperit non esse conveniens. Oportet enim veram matrem de eadem esse essentia qua est ex se natum; ferri tamen posse propter ipsam considerationem, et quod solum nominetur de Virgine hoc verbum propter inseparabile templum Dei Verbi ex ipsa, non quia ipsa sit mater Dei Verbi; nemo enim antiquiorem se parit.

7. Haec quidem existimo praecedentem famam significasse; exponimus vero etiam nos quae contigerunt, et rebus ostendimus quia fraterno animo negotium eorum quos praediximus nosse cupimus, non desiderio curiositatis importunae, cum et nostra narremus, tamquam fratres fratribus, novitatem sectarum nobis invicem publicantes, ut sit mihi principium litterarum verissimum: dixi enim,

cum has litteras inciperem, quia fraternas invicem debemus collocutiones. Omnem quae tecum est in Christo fraternitatem ego et qui mecum sunt salutamus.

EPISTOLA II NESTORII AD COELESTINUM PAPAM.

1. Saepe scripsi beatitudini tuae propter Julianum, Orontium, et caeteros, qui sibi usurpant episcopalem dignitatem, et creberrimam aditionem apud piissimum et praedicatissimum imperatorem faciunt, nosque concidunt frequentibus lamentationibus, tamquam temporibus orthodoxis de Occidente projecti. At huc usque scripta de his a tua veneratione non suscepimus: quae si haberem, possem eis respondere, daremque compendiosum responsum vocibus eorum. Nunc enim ab incertis dictis eorum, non habet quis ad quod se convertat: aliis haereticos eos vocantibus, et ideo de Occidentalibus partibus projectos esse dicentibus: ipsis vero jurantibus, calumniam se sustinuisse, et periculum pro orthodoxa fide ex subreptione perpessos. Quorum utrum certum sit, nobis gravis est ignorantia: nam condolere eis, si vere haeretici sunt, crimen est; et iterum non condolere, si calumniam sustinent, durum et impium est.

2. Dignetur igitur amantissima Dei anima tua informare nos, qui ad utrumque momentum huc usque dividimur, id est, et ad odium et ad miserationem eorum; doceri autem volumus, quam de his sententiam teneamus. Differimus enim eosdem viros per dies singulos dissimulantes, spe et exspectatione beatitudinis tuae.

3. Non est enim, o venerandissime, sicut nosti res vilis discussio piae sectae: nec parva est probatio eorum, qui hoc agunt. Multus enim etiam nobis labor hic celebratur, dum elaboramus eruere sordidissimam impietatem pessimae opinionis Apollinaris et Arii de Ecclesia Dei: nescio enim quemadmodum quidam de ecclesiasticis, quamdam contemperationis imaginem ex deitate et humanitate Unigeniti concipientes, aegrotent aegritudine praedictorum haereticorum: dum et corporis passiones audent superfundere deitati Unigeniti, et immutabilitatem deitatis ad naturam corporis transiisse

confingunt, et utramque naturam (quae per conjunctionem summam et inconfusam in una persona Unigeniti adoratur) contemperationis mutabilitate confundunt.

4. Caeci, qui nec sanctorum illorum Patrum expositionem meminerunt, nec vident aperte adversus eos reclamantes: Credimus in unum Dominum Jesum Christum filium Dei incarnatum ex Spiritu sancto et Maria virgine. Haec enim vox, in Dominum, significat utramque naturam; etenim Christus est deitati Patris ὁμούσιος: humanitas vero posterioribus temporibus nata ex sancta Virgine, propter conjunctionem deitatis ab angelis et hominibus simul colitur.

5. Eum ergo, qui hic propter sectarum pravitatem tot laboribus fatigatur, considera, quid iterum pati necesse est, si negotium praedictorum virorum nesciat, timeatque nimis, ne additamentum haereticorum per ignorantiam hic positus faciat. Unde rogo, ut undique studiosum sit sanctae animae tuae, donare notitiam praedictorum virorum: maxime cum litterarum sequester fidelissimus Valerius cubicularius possit beatitudini tuae per se exponere molestias eorum. Omnem in Christo fraternitatem, quae tecum est, ego et qui mecum sunt, plurimum salutamus.

EPISTOLA III NESTORII AD COELESTIUM RESCRIBENTIS.

Honorabili et religiosissimo presbytero Coelstio Nestorius in Domino salutem.

1. Noli aegre ferre, venerabilis, perferens ab his qui ea quae inferuntur facere debent, et praesertim asserentibus veritatem, et refugientibus pollutorum vel contaminatorum communionem: quia et sanctis, qui ante nostram aetatem exstiterunt, gratae fuerunt aerumnae; et ipsae quidem temporales erant, veritas autem aeterna. Sic Joannes Baptista de peccato arguens Herodem, et quidem regem existentem, capite condemnatus est; sed non formidavit, Christum enim habebat caput quod non posset abscindi. Sic Paulus hoc modo quoque et Petrus sunt interfecti. Et quid amplius dici opus est? Ita actum est semper, per diversas tentationes pietate currente.

2. Noli igitur a veritate deficiens eam prodere (siquidem epistolae missae episcopis a concilio Occidentis, et ab Alexandrino, multis rescriptis manifestam nobis nostram fecere sententiam), prudentibus scilicet ejusdem orthodoxae professionis: forsitan enim utile aliquid Ecclesiis rectae fidei proveniet, Domino cooperante. Omnem fraternitatem salutamus.

Et alia manu: Incolumis et forti animo, et plurimum orans pro nobis, doneris nobis, religiosissime frater.

The Scriptorium Project is the work of a small group of lay people of various apostolic churches who are interested in the preservation, transmission, and translation of the works of the early and medieval church. Our efforts are to make the works of the church fathers accessible to anyone who might have an interest in Christian antiquities and the theological, philosophical, and moral writings that have become the bedrock of Western Civilization.

To-date, our releases have pulled from the Greek, Syriac, Georgian, Latin, Celtic, Ethiopian, and Coptic traditions of Christianity, and have been pulled from sundry local traditions and languages.

Other Selections from the Byzantine Church Series:

Sermons by Nestorius of Constantinople (May 2009)

Theophrastus by Aeneas of Gaza (Apr. 2011)

Treatise on Prayer by St. Evargius of Ponticus (May 2011)

The Lausiac History by St. Palladius of Galatia (Mar. 2013)

Letter on the Fall of Constantinople by Isidore of Kiev (Oct. 2013)

Selected Laws by Justinian I, Emperor of Rome (July 2018)

Exhortation to Monks Ordained in India by St. John of Karpathos (March 2021)

Fragments of 'Chronicle' by Hippolytus of Thebes (May 2023)

The Life of the Blessed Theotokos by Epiphanius Monachus (July 2023)

Letters of Nestorius by Nestorius of Constantinople (Sept. 2023)

www.ingramcontent.com/pod-product-compliance
Lightning Source LLC
LaVergne TN
LVHW010424070526
838199LV00064B/5413